A Mother's Perspective

Have I ever told how much I love watching you play with your friends? Soccer in the front yard; movies on the couch; that competitive fire on the field; the playful silliness of little boys.

I smile and giggle inside each time I watch you "hanging" with the boys, developing into the young man I know you will become.

I melt with joy when I see you choose what is right and display to others the values and morals I hope I have instilled in you through my words and actions.

I love that you still ask me to snuggle with you at bedtime. Whether we are reading your latest book or doing cross word puzzles or talking, this is my favorite time of day! These times have given me some of the best insight into who you will become…your dreams, your likes and dislikes, your friends and even those that are only "so called friends".

I also am very aware that before I know it, the day will come when you no longer want to snuggle with me. You will be too grown to have mommy read you stories and give you hugs. But, until then, I enjoy every minute!!

My fear is that those conversations filled with information about your day other than "fine" and "nothing" will end. The time we spend together sharing silly stories, pondering "why" and "how" the world is the way it is, will be replaced. The conversation will be reduced to eye-rolling, a shrugging of shoulders and maybe a negative tone of voice. You may even think that you don't need me anymore!

As long as you know that I am always here for you, I will have to come to terms with the growing up process. I cannot keep you as my little boy, chasing the puppy around the yard, giddy with happiness, forever. I keep those memories locked away in my heart for safe keeping. But, the memories do not need to end as you grow. New ones will, of course, take shape and the conversations will change from soccer goals, video games and homework to college, girls, and the future.

In order to keep the conversation going now, I want to suggest we begin writing to one another in this journal. It may seem silly at first but I hope it will not only keep the conversation going but spark new ones. What if you want to ask me something about your new teenage body but feel embarrassed? Or about the girl who just asked you to the prom? Maybe you want to just tell me about your day and vent about school but don't really want me to answer you?

Our relationship has always been different than anyone else in the house. Tough love maybe; my fierce love and strong conviction towards you is bigger than me. I know that by being the best mother to you that I possibly can be, I am impacting more than just one small child, more than just one little boy trying to spread his wings; more than one unruly teenager. I am hard on you for the husband that you will become; for the employee and maybe employer that you will develop into and most importantly, for the father of children, ideas, and history that you will produce.

"Men are what their mothers made them." ~ Ralph Waldo Emerson

I know that I am creating all of this with my words and actions and therefore, they mean so much more to me than just simple gibberish or meaningless activities.

This is why I want to keep the conversation going; to be your sounding board on paper; to share with you how my heart aches when you are hurting; to help you understand and always remember that you are not alone but yet have support and encouragement whenever you want or need it.

JUST MOM & ME

A MOTHER - SON JOURNAL

www.onefam.com

Your Family Story

Founded in 2016, OneFam is the easy way to discover, preserve and relive your family history anywhere anytime. OneFam aims to make family history available to as many families as possible. Our suite of products include Journals, Family Tree Software (web, mobile and desktop), Ancestry DNA Testing and Family History Research. Connect, share and protect your family history for generations to come.

ONE·FAM

Visit us at onefam.com

This Journal Belongs to:

_____

_____

_____

Date Journal Starts:

_____

Journal Guidelines

First and foremost, the purpose of this shared journal is…..
HAVE FUN!!! Before we begin, let's set some guidelines for sharing.

1) This should be a memorable, fun and most importantly, stress free way of sharing. If you feel it is no longer FUN and you feel it's not of benefit, let's talk about it!

2) Be Yourself! I want you to share, laugh, be silly, serious, crazy, passionate or sad. Whatever makes you, YOU!

3) Judgement Free Zone. Consider this to be a safe place to share, ask, discuss, tell whatever it is that you are thinking or feeling. If you do not want to discuss it further, just make a little note that says "No Talk" somewhere on the page.

4) Who should be able to read it? If this is just between you and I, then let's leave it that way. No one else needs to read what we write.

5) How often should we write? This can be a spur of the moment or a routine.

6) Where? How will the other one know where to read the journal? Shall we pick a "reading" place where we will pick it up?

7) Does every entry require a response? Sometimes we may just want to vent, or share, without requiring a response. How should we let the other person know that there is no need to "say" anything?

8) Have fun!!! This one is so important that it just needed to be said again.

HAPPY WRITING!

"Men are what their mothers made them."

Ralph Waldo Emerson

"Moms are as relentless as the tides. They just don't drive us to practice, they drive us to greatness."

Steve Rushin

Name:

Nickname:

Birthday:

Star Sign:

Eye Color:

Hair Color:

Height:

Mother

Son Details

Name:

Nickname:

Birthday:

Star Sign:

Eye Color:

Hair Color:

Height:

Date:

Insert Photo

Picture of Mom

Date: _____

Insert Photo

Picture of Son

Date: _____

10 Reasons I Love My Son

1:

2:

3:

4:

5:

6:

7:

8:

9:

10:

10 Reasons I Love My Mother

1: ....

2: ....

3: ....

4: ....

5: ....

6: ....

7: ....

8: ....

9: ....

10: ....

Date: _____

A story about when I was a little girl: ....

Date: ....

Story Time

A story about when I was a little boy:

....

....

....

....

....

....

....

....

....

....

....

....

....

....

....

....

....

....

....

....

Date: _____

Son

5 Favorite Places & Why

1: ....
....
....
....
....

2: ....
....
....
....
....

3: ....
....
....
....
....

4: ....
....
....
....
....

5: ....
....
....
....
....

Date: _____

5 Favorite Places & Why

1: ....
....
....
....

2: ....
....
....
....

3: ....
....
....
....

4: ....
....
....
....

5: ....
....
....
....

Date: _____

Somethings I wish we talked about: ....

....

....

....

....

....

....

Things my mother talked to me about: ....

....

....

....

Things I wished my mother had talked to me about: ....

....

....

....

....

....

The first boy I had a crush on: ....

....

....

....

Date: _____

Son Talk

Things I would like to talk about now: ....
....
....
....
....
....
....

Things I'm not yet ready to talk about: ....
....
....
....
....
....
....

The first girl I had a crush on: ....
....
....
....
....
....
....
....

Date: _____

10 Favorite Songs

Date: _____

10 Favorite Songs

Date: _____

"There has never been, nor will there ever be, anything quite so special as the love between the mother and a son."

Author Unknown

"A man loves his sweetheart the most, his wife the best, but his mother the longest."

Old Irish Proverb

10 Favorite Books

1:

2:

3:

4:

5:

6:

7:

8:

9:

10:

Date:

10 Favorite Books

1:

2:

3:

4:

5:

6:

7:

8:

9:

10:

Son

Date: _____

5 Books I Wish You Would Read

Mother ★

1: ....
....
....
....

2: ....
....
....
....

3: ....
....
....
....

4: ....
....
....
....

5: ....
....
....
....

Date: _____

5 Books I Wish You Would Read

1:
....
....
....
....

2:
....
....
....
....

3:
....
....
....
....

4:
....
....
....
....

5:
....
....
....
....

Date: _____

Drawing of the Happiest Day

Draw a picture of the happiest day you remember.

Date: _____

Drawing of the Happiest Day

Draw a picture of the happiest day you remember.

Insert Photo

A picture of us doing something
we love together.

Date: _____

Insert Photo

A picture of us doing something
we love together.

Date: _____

About: ....
....

Story: ....

....

....

....

....

....

....

....

....

....

....

....

....

....

....

....

....

....

....

Mother

Date: _____

Tell Me a Story

About: ....
....

Story: ....
....
....
....
....
....
....
....
....
....
....
....
....
....
....
....
....
....
....
....
....

Son

Date: _____

A description of how life was growing up as a child:

Mother

Date:

Childhood Memories

A description of how life was growing up as a child:

Date:

Son

My 5 Best Friends & Why

1:
....
....
....
....

2:
....
....
....
....

3:
....
....
....
....

4:
....
....
....
....

5:
....
....
....
....

My 5 Best Friends & Why

1:

2:

3:

4:

5:

Date: _____

Mother

What causes problems between us:

How I act when I'm annoyed or angry with you:

How I wish you would respond:

How I could respond better:

Date:

Feelings & Emotions

What causes problems between us:

How I act when I'm annoyed or angry with you:

How I wish you would respond:

How I could respond better:

Date:

How I feel during an argument:

How I feel after an argument:

How I try to fix things afterwards:

Mother

Date:

Feelings & Emotions

How I feel during an argument:

How I feel after an argument:

How I try to fix things afterwards:

Date:

Mother's Notes

Date: _____

Son's Notes

Date: _____

Mother

Date: _____

Remember That Time....

Date: _____

Things to Do Together - Bucket List

1:

2:

3:

4:

5:

6:

7:

8:

9:

10:

Things to Do Together - Bucket List

1:

2:

3:

4:

5:

6:

7:

8:

9:

10:

Date:

Tell Me a Story

About: ....
....

Story: ....
....
....
....
....
....
....
....
....
....
....
....
....
....
....
....
....
....
....
....

Mother

Date: _____

Tell Me a Story

About:

Story:

Son

Date: _____

My 5 Earliest Childhood Memories

1: ....
....
....
....

2: ....
....
....
....
....

3: ....
....
....
....

4: ....
....
....
....

5: ....
....
....
....

Date: _____

My 5 Earliest Childhood Memories

1: ....
....
....
....
....

2: ....
....
....
....
....

3: ....
....
....
....
....

4: ....
....
....
....
....

5: ....
....
....
....
....

Date: _____

Insert Photo

Find a photo from
your childhood.

Date: _____

Insert Photo

Find a photo from
your childhood.

Date: _____

Things You Don't Know About Me

1:

2:

3:

4:

5:

6:

7:

8:

9:

10:

Mother

Date: _____

Things You Don't Know About Me

....

....

1: ....

....

2: ....

....

3: ....

....

4: ....

....

5: ....

....

6: ....

....

7: ....

....

8: ....

....

9: ....

....

10: ....

....

....

....

....

Date: _____

★ Son

Mother

What I wanted to be growing up:

Jobs I worked in and why:

What I would like for my son in 5 years:

te:

Dreams & Goals

What I wanted to be growing up:

....

....

....

....

Jobs I would like to have in the future:

....

....

....

....

....

....

....

....

What I would like for my mother in 5 years:

....

....

....

....

....

....

....

....

....

Date: _____

Dreams & Goals

Where I would like to be in 5 years:

....
....
....
....
....
....
....

Where I would like to be in 10 years:

....
....
....
....
....
....
....

What I wish I had done 10 years ago:

....
....
....
....
....
....

Date: _____

Dreams & Goals

Where I would like to be in 5 years:

....

....

....

....

....

....

Where I would like to be in 10 years:

....

....

....

....

....

....

Where I would like to be in 15 years:

....

....

....

....

....

....

Date: _____

★ Son

Draw a picture of the world in 100 years time.

Date: _____

Drawing of Life in the Future

Draw a picture of the world in 100 years time.

"There is an endearing tenderness in the love of a mother to a son that transcends all other affections of the heart."

Washington Irving

"A good son will never allow sorrow to befall her mother... and act as if he is an only child that cares...protects when no one dares...serves with his life in return...and most of all finds a wife that will love his mother too.

Helen RebibisS Ramo

My Greatest Accomplishments

1:

2:

3:

4:

5:

6:

7:

8:

9:

10:

My Greatest Accomplishments

1:

2:

3:

4:

5:

6:

7:

8:

9:

10:

Date: _____

Details of my education:

How I feel about my education:

What I wish I had done differently:

Things I would like to help you with:

Date:

Education

Why do you think education is important:

....

....

....

....

How do you feel about your grades:

....

....

....

....

What you can do to improve:

....

....

....

....

....

Things you would like more help with:

....

....

....

....

Date: _____

Insert Photo

A picture of your first day at
school or college.

Date: _____

Insert Photo

A picture of your first day at
school or college.

Date: _____

Times You Made Me Proud

1: ....
....
....
....
....

2: ....
....
....
....
....

3: ....
....
....
....

4: ....
....
....
....
....

5: ....
....
....
....

Date: _____

Mother

Times You Made Me Proud

1: ....
....
....
....

2: ....
....
....
....

3: ....
....
....
....

4: ....
....
....
....

5: ....
....
....
....

Date: _____

Son

Draw/illustrate or write the things that show your love.

Date: _____

How Do You Know I Love You

Draw/illustrate or write the things that show your love.

About: ....
....

Story: ....

....

....

....

....

....

....

....

....

....

....

....

....

....

....

....

....

....

....

....

Date: _____

Mother

Tell Me a Story

About: ....

....

Story: ....

....

....

....

....

....

....

....

....

....

....

....

....

....

....

....

....

....

....

....

....

....

Date: _____

Son

My Biggest Regrets in Life

1:
....
....
....

2:
....
....
....

3:
....
....
....

4:
....
....
....

5:
....
....
....

What I have learned from my regrets:
....
....
....
....

Date: _____

My Biggest Regrets in Life

1:

2:

3:

4:

5:

What I have learned from my regrets:

Date:

Insert Photo

My Favorite Photo of

us together

Date: _____

Insert Photo

My Favorite Photo of

us together

Date: _____

Mother

Date: _____

Son's Notes

Date: _____

10 Things I Love

1:

2:

3:

4:

5:

6:

7:

8:

9:

10:

10 Things I Love

1:

2:

3:

4:

5:

6:

7:

8:

9:

10:

Date: _____

Son

10 Things I Hate

1:

2:

3:

4:

5:

6:

7:

8:

9:

10:

Date:

10 Things I Hate

1:

2:

3:

4:

5:

6:

7:

8:

9:

10:

Date: _____

Mother

Date: _____

Remember That Time....

Date: _____

If I Had 3 Wishes

Mother

1: ....

....

....

....

Date: ....

....

....

....

2: ....

....

....

....

....

....

....

....

3: ....

....

....

....

....

....

....

Date: _____

If I had 3 Wishes

1: ....
....
....
....
....
....
....
....

2: ....
....
....
....
....
....
....

3: ....
....
....
....
....
....

Date: _____

Son

"Even more than the time when she gave birth, a mother feels her greatest joy when she hears others refer to her son as a wise learned one."

Thiruvalluvar

"A man never sees all that his mother has been to him until it's too late to let her know that he sees it."

W. D. Howells

Tell Me a Story

Mother

About:

Story:

...te:

Tell Me a Story

About: ....
....

Story: ....

....
....
....
....
....
....
....
....
....
....
....
....
....
....
....
....
....
....
....
....
....
....

Date: _____

Son

Draw a picture of an item, object or place you like.

Drawing of Something I Like

Draw a picture of an item, object or place you like.

Why We are the Same

Why We are Different

Date: _____

Why We are the Same

Date:

Why We are Different

Date: _____

Describe Your Son

Date: _____

Describe Your Mother

Date: _____

Mother

Date: _____

Funny Things You Have Said or Done

Son

Date: _____

Mother

What is your favorite color?

What is your shoe size?

What city were you born in?

What is your favorite dessert and why?

What is your favorite movie & why?

What is your favorite TV series and why?

Date: _____

Quick Questions

What is your favorite color?

What is your shoe size?

What city were you born in?

What is your favorite dessert and why?

What is your favorite movie & why?

What is your favorite TV series and why?

Date:

If you could visit any place in the world, where would it be and why?

If you could travel back in time to one moment, what would that moment be and why?

What is your favorite possession in the world?

What is your favorite season?

Date:

Quick Questions

If you could visit any place in the world, where would it be and why?

If you could change anything about your life, what would it be?

What is your favorite possession in the world?

What is your favorite season?

Date:

Drawing of A Memory

Draw a picture of a memory you cherish.

Date: _____

Drawing of A Memory

Draw a picture of a memory you cherish.

5 Best Things About You

1: ....
....
....
....
....

2: ....
....
....
....
....

3: ....
....
....
....
....

4: ....
....
....
....
....

5: ....
....
....
....
....

Date: _____

Mother

5 Best Things About You

1: ....
....
....
....

2: ....
....
....
....

3: ....
....
....
....

4: ....
....
....
....

5: ....
....
....
....

Date: _____

5 Things You Do That Annoy Me

Mother

1:

2:

3:

4:

5:

5 Things You Do That Annoy Me

1: ....
....
....
....
....

2: ....
....
....
....
....

3: ....
....
....
....
....

4: ....
....
....
....
....

5: ....
....
....
....
....

Date: _____

★ Son

Write down the recipe for your favorite food.

Date:

Recipe for Favorite Food We Make

Write down the recipe for your favorite food.

Date: _____

About:

Story:

Mother

Date: _____

Tell Me a Story

About: ....
....

Story: ....
....
....
....
....
....
....
....
....
....
....
....
....
....
....
....
....
....
....
....
....
....
....
....
....

Son

Date: _____

Write the details of your family holidays, the locations and favorite mother/son memories from the holiday.

Mother

Date: _____

Family Holidays

Write the details of your family holidays, the locations and favorite mother/son memories from the holiday.

Date: _____

Insert Photo

A picture of us on a
family holiday

Date: _____

Insert Photo

A picture of us on a
family holiday

Date: _____

"Youth fades; love droops; the leaves of friendship fall; A mother's secret hope outlives them all."

Oliver Wendell Holmes

"A wise son makes a glad father, But a foolish son is the grief of his mother... A wise son makes a father glad, But a foolish man despises his mother."

The Proverbs of Solomon

Mother

Date: _____

Remember That Time....

Son

Date: _____

Insert Photo

Photos of us at the same age

Date: _____

Insert Photo

Photos of us at the same age

Date: _____

Mother

What sports and hobbies interest you?

Would you like to share any of the above with your son?

.te:

Sports & Hobbies

What sports and hobbies interest you?

....

....

....

....

....

....

....

....

....

....

Would you like to share any of the above with your mother?

....

....

....

....

....

....

....

Date: _____

Mother

Date: _____

What Did You Learn from this Journal

Date: _____

Mother

Date:

Son's Notes

Date: _____

Son

Mother

Date: _____

Son's Notes

Date: _____

Mother

Date: _____

Son's Notes

Date: _____

Mother's Notes

Mother

Date: _____

Son's Notes

Date: _____

Mother

Date: _____

Son's Notes

Date: _____

Sign Up to OneFam

At OneFam we aim to make family history available to everyone. We would like to invite you to become a member of OneFam community and enjoy exclusive benefits. With already over 25,000 users worldwide, we promise you'll be in good company.

- 50% off your next journal purchases
- Access to free family tree software
- Birthday gifts
- Free shipping offers
- First dibs on sales
- & more...

To subscribe, simply visit our website at:

https://www.onefam.com/subscribe/

ONE FAM

Create Your Family Free

Get started with your free online family tree in minutes. Simply sign up, add your parents, siblings, children, grandparents and other family members.

- Preserve Images, Videos, Audio, Stories & Events
- Invite & Connect with Family Members
- Create and Share Family History
- Available on Web, Mobile and Ipad

ONE FAM

www.onefam.com

More Great Journals

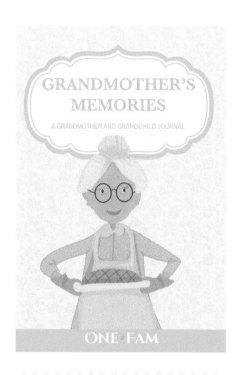

GRANDMOTHER'S MEMORIES

A GRANDMOTHER AND GRANDCHILD JOURNAL

ONE·FAM

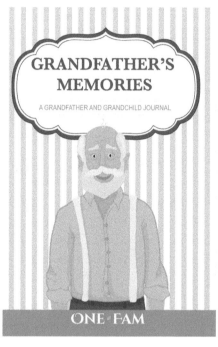

GRANDFATHER'S MEMORIES

A GRANDFATHER AND GRANDCHILD JOURNAL

ONE·FAM

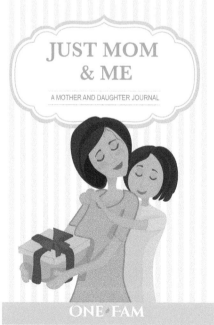

JUST MOM & ME

A MOTHER AND DAUGHTER JOURNAL

ONE·FAM

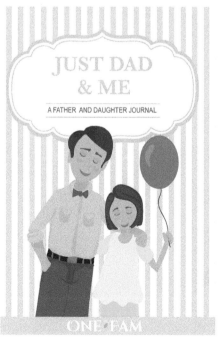

JUST DAD & ME

A FATHER AND DAUGHTER JOURNAL

ONE·FAM

Visit Onefam.com for our full range

More Great Journals

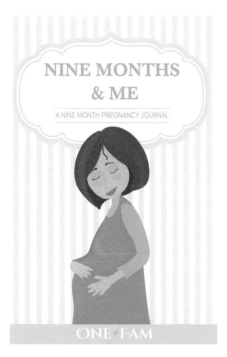

CPSIA information can be obtained
at www.ICGtesting.com
Printed in the USA
LVHW020410150119
603811LV00022B/708/P

9 781999 893712